The Collaboration Cards

Increase collaboration by the minute and destroy this book along the way

Alistair Cockburn

©Alistair Cockburn 2025 all rights reserved
ISBN: 979-8-9985862-2-4 paperback
Humans and Technology Press
5325 20th Ave S
Gulfport, FL 33707
v1.1 20250520-1103

For more on The Collaboration Cards:
https://collaborationcards.com/

See other books by Alistair Cockburn:
https://alistaircockburn.com/Books

1997   Surviving Object Oriented Projects
2000   Writing Effective Use Cases
2001   Agile Software Development (1st ed)
2002   Patterns for Effective Use Cases
2003   People and Methodologies in Software
       Development (Dr. Philos.)
2004   Crystal Clear: A human-powered
       methodology for small teams
2006   Agile Software Development: The
       cooperative game (2nd ed)
2021   Design in Object Technology: Class of 1994
2022   Design in Object Technology: The
       Annotated Class of 1994
2022   Love Trio Trio del Amor (poems)
2024   Unifying User Stories, Use Cases, Story
       Maps (preview ed.)
2025   Hexagonal Architecture Explained

Destroy this book

A book only serves its purpose when it's being used. These cards, to be useful, need to be in your hands — one at a time or as a full deck. As long as they're bound inside this book, they're hard to use.

I tried printing cards. They're expensive to print and ship, and they don't travel easily around the world. Books, however, are inexpensive and widely available. Hence: a book.

But don't leave the cards trapped inside. Tear them out. Destroy the binding. Don't worry about preserving the "book" — free the cards.

Then use them.

A brief history

Collaboration is a "dance of contribution."

In 2007, I was asked to contribute an article about collaboration. Not having particular expertise on the subject, I sent out a questionnaire asking friends and colleagues to share moments when they saw collaboration improve.

From their anecdotes, I distilled out the specific actions people took that enhanced the atmosphere for collaboration.

From that research, I wrote the article
"Collaboration: The dance of contribution"
[https://web.archive.org/web/20140329201744/http://alistair.cockburn.us/Collaboration:+the+dance+of+contribution].

You can even read the raw notes, if you want to find new patterns yourself:
[https://web.archive.org/web/20140329203525/http://alistair.cockburn.us/Collaboration,+the+Dance+of+Contribution,+raw+notes].

The article was hard to put into practice, so in 2010 I created the first batch of "Collaboration Cards": [https://web.archive.org/web/20140329205710/http://alistair.cockburn.us/Collaboration+Cards].

Over the years, and with the help and constant prodding by Sole Pinter, the cards evolved, growing and shrinking depending on the printing costs, until I ended up with the set you now hold.

These cards give you a **vocabulary for collaboration**. As you practice tuning your senses to them, you will see them happening everywhere. That makes these cards unique, and why I want you to use them.

Take a look online for the card decks: https://collaborationcards.com/

How to use them

Here are 6 starter ideas for using them. I encourage you to find more.

1: "One a day"

Each day, pick up a card, either at random or work your way through the deck. Carry it in front of you all day long.

Notice when people enact that card's action, and notice when they violate it. Just notice, nothing more.

You are tuning your senses to pick up the vocabulary of collaboration. Over time, you will notice and be able to name them without having the card in your hands.

Then, of course, you can start to enact that card yourself: *Lower your relative social position, Add humor, Recognize others,* and so on.

2: "Team theme"

Similar to "One-a-day," but for a team.

The team selects one card to practice as their theme for a week.

Each person watches for uses of the card during the week.

Unlike the personal One-a-day, they are not looking for when it is violated (well, they might notice, but they have to keep quiet about it). Rather, they are looking to call out whenever someone enacts the card.

They generate public positive feedback enacting that card, bringing use of it into everyone's awareness. "What you focus on, expands," as they say.

3: "Top card"

Good for groups whose members know each other, such as a family or work group.

One person, the "it" person, chooses the one *card* that they feel they use the most easily, their most natural way of acting in a collaborative setting.

(This, alone, is a great way for people to introduce themselves in a new team.)

Everyone else also chooses a card for that person, what they feel is that person's way of contributing in a collaborative moment.

When everyone has chosen a card, the "it" person reads their card. Then everyone else shows what they had chosen for that person. The "it" person is likely to be surprised at how different the other people's perceptions are. It's a lovely gift.

Continue around the team, each person being the "it" person in turn.

4: "The lonely card"

Find the card you use the *least*, or struggle enacting.

Decide where you are on a scale of 0-10. Zero means you have never ever used it, 1 means you used it once, 2 means occasionally, and so on up to 10, where it is your natural behavior. It's likely you'll place yourself at a two or three, since this is the card you use the least.

First, just carry it around, as in One-a-day. Look to notice anyone else using it, and notice how they use it.

Then, see if you can use it just enough to go up *1* point on your scale. Not two points or five points, just *1* point.

When you have accomplished that, put the card back in the deck. You're done for now.

This activity can be done by a single person or as a team theme.

5: "Yellow card on the field!"

This is not for everyone: It is very revealing and can be used to attack someone, which is not the point. It may be useful for executives looking to improve their managing and collaboration style, or to analyze someone in a coaching context. Be careful with it.

Choose the card that you *violate* the most, the one that you occasionally or habitually do the opposite of.

For example, *"Inquire, don't contradict."* You might have a habit of contradicting someone else's ideas, which shuts them down.

Reveal to selected people what your "yellow card" is. They get to say "Yellow card on the field!" when your action violates that card. (A yellow card is given in soccer for a rule infraction, hence the name.)

You can see why this is both dangerous, and useful for certain people. Use with care.

6: "Problem solving"

With some people to help you brainstorm and analyze, name a problem you are wrestling with.

Go through the cards and name which cards, if you started using them more, would help resolve or improve the problem situation.

This activity works well in a coaching or consulting setting, if you draft some friends to help you, or in a workshop where you don't know the other people. It's amazing how others can help you see how improving collaboration in various ways can help your situation.

This activity is thanks to and courtesy of Sole Pinter, who invented it and used it with great effect.

7: "My way"

Describe your own way of using the cards.

And if you like, send it to me so I can add it to the catalog: totheralistair@aol.com.

Chapter 3. The cards.

The following pages are meant to be torn out and turned into individual cards.

 (Yes, I could print the cards – but they are expensive and hard to ship. I wanted to make a book with perforated pages for you to tear out, but the minimum size was 6"x9", which is too large. All of which is why you have this book in your hands and are now going to tear the pages out.)

I leave the last page in the book blank, because you're going to find your own idea for what improves collaboration by the minute, and you're going to want to write it down.

Here are the five suits, summarized, followed by the individual cards.

Suit 1: Lift Others

- ✓ Recognize others
- ✓ Inquire, don't contradict
- ✓ Challenge but adopt
- ✓ Lower your relative social position

Suit 2: Increase Safety

- ✓ Show you won't hurt
- ✓ Be yourself
- ✓ Say something honest at the edge of what you think is allowed
- ✓ Add humor

Suit 3: Get Results

✓ Say something valuable
✓ Get back from diversions
✓ Clarify the way forward
✓ Get one result

Suit 4: Add Energy

- ✓ Contribute
- ✓ Keep your energy high
- ✓ Challenge
- ✓ Make it fun

Suit 5: Lift Yourself

- ✓ Find your center
- ✓ Raise your own sense of power

COLLABORATION

The Dance of Contribution

Lift Others

Recognize others

Ask for their thoughts,
accept an idea. When you build
on their idea, let them know,
so they get recognition.

Delight in the ways they find
to implement their ideas.

LIFT OTHERS

COLLABORATION

The Dance of
Contribution

Lift
Others

Inquire, don't contradict

When inclined to contradict, inquire instead, to discover new information that makes the answer other than what you expected.

Work to understand why the other person's answer is so different.

LIFT OTHERS

© Alistair Cockburn, 2018
http://CollaborationCards.com

COLLABORATION

The Dance of Contribution

Lift Others

Challenge but adopt

It is uplifting when someone disagrees with you at first, but then sees and adopts your view.

Do this for someone else. Look to adopt their ideas where possible, so they know they are heard and their ideas valued.

LIFT OTHERS

© Alistair Cockburn, 2018
http://CollaborationCards.com

COLLABORATION

The Dance of Contribution

Lift Others

Lower your relative social position

By tone of voice and gesture, place the other person at your same level or higher.

This includes self-deprecating humor. It does not mean groveling.

LIFT OTHERS

COLLABORATION

The Dance of Contribution

Increase Safety

Show you won't hurt

Show that you won't say things that hurt the other person. With someone to back up and protect them, they might feel brave enough to step in.

Leave some privacy. If there is nowhere safe to hide, fear goes up, safety goes down. Don't leak information that will hurt. This should be obvious.

INCREASE SAFETY

© Alistair Cockburn, 2018
http://CollaborationCards.com

COLLABORATION

The Dance of Contribution

Increase Safety

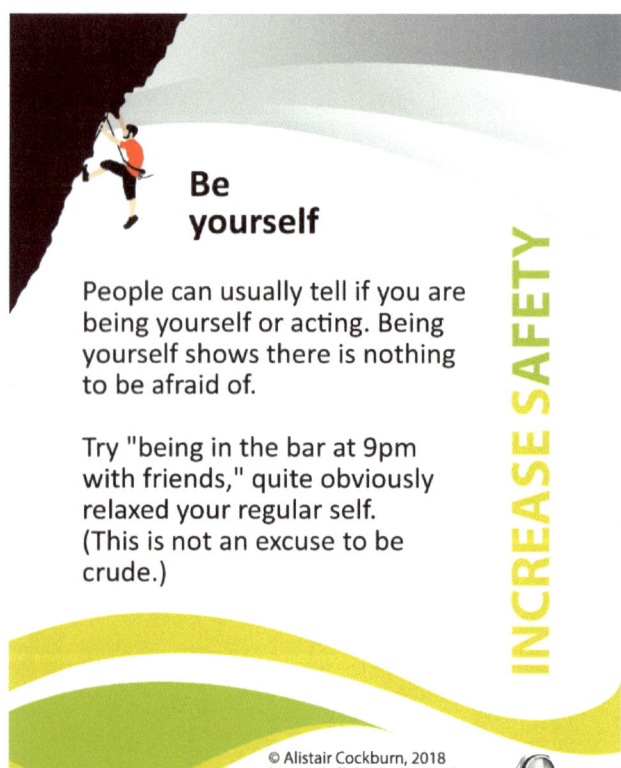

Be yourself

People can usually tell if you are being yourself or acting. Being yourself shows there is nothing to be afraid of.

Try "being in the bar at 9pm with friends," quite obviously relaxed your regular self. (This is not an excuse to be crude.)

INCREASE SAFETY

© Alistair Cockburn, 2018
http://CollaborationCards.com

COLLABORATION

The Dance of Contribution

Increase Safety

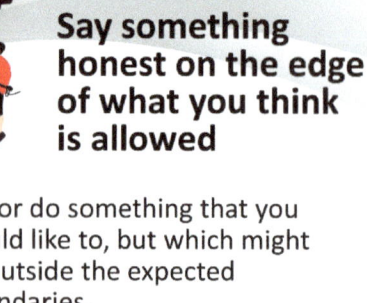

Say something honest on the edge of what you think is allowed

Say or do something that you would like to, but which might lie outside the expected boundaries.

This widens the boundaries. What others were afraid to say or do may suddenly appear "safe" to them.

INCREASE SAFETY

© Alistair Cockburn, 2018
http://CollaborationCards.com

COLLABORATION

The Dance of Contribution

Increase Safety

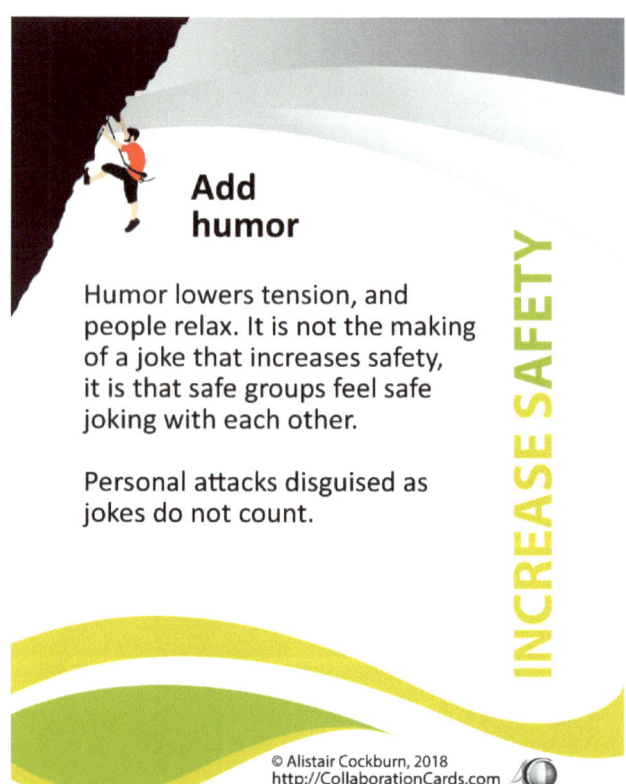

Add humor

Humor lowers tension, and people relax. It is not the making of a joke that increases safety, it is that safe groups feel safe joking with each other.

Personal attacks disguised as jokes do not count.

INCREASE SAFETY

COLLABORATION

The Dance of Contribution

Get Results

Say something valuable

Try to make your first speaking of value.

This moves the work forward, and it encourages others to listen to you.

GET RESULTS

COLLABORATION

The Dance of Contribution

Get Results

Get back from diversions

Keep your ideas on topic.

Going off track for a little while releases some tension in the room, but people appreciate being brought back.

GET RESULTS

COLLABORATION

The Dance of Contribution

Get Results

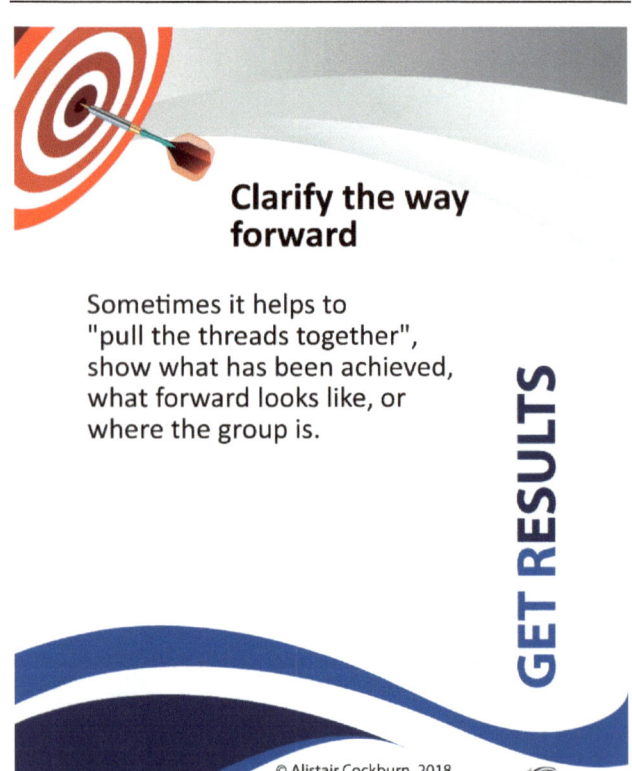

Clarify the way forward

Sometimes it helps to "pull the threads together", show what has been achieved, what forward looks like, or where the group is.

GET RESULTS

COLLABORATION

The Dance of Contribution

Get Results

Get one result

Getting a result is heartening.

Good facilitators often generate a victory to help encourage and bind the group.

If the session is ending, aim for a small goal, so that the group can end with a victory.

GET RESULTS

COLLABORATION

The Dance of Contribution

Add Energy

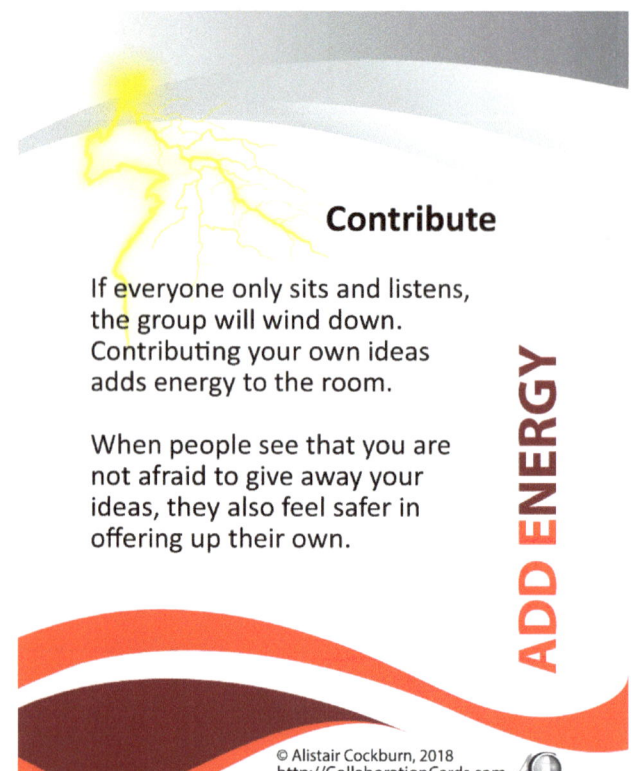

Contribute

If everyone only sits and listens, the group will wind down. Contributing your own ideas adds energy to the room.

When people see that you are not afraid to give away your ideas, they also feel safer in offering up their own.

ADD ENERGY

© Alistair Cockburn, 2018
http://CollaborationCards.com

COLLABORATION

The Dance of Contribution

Add Energy

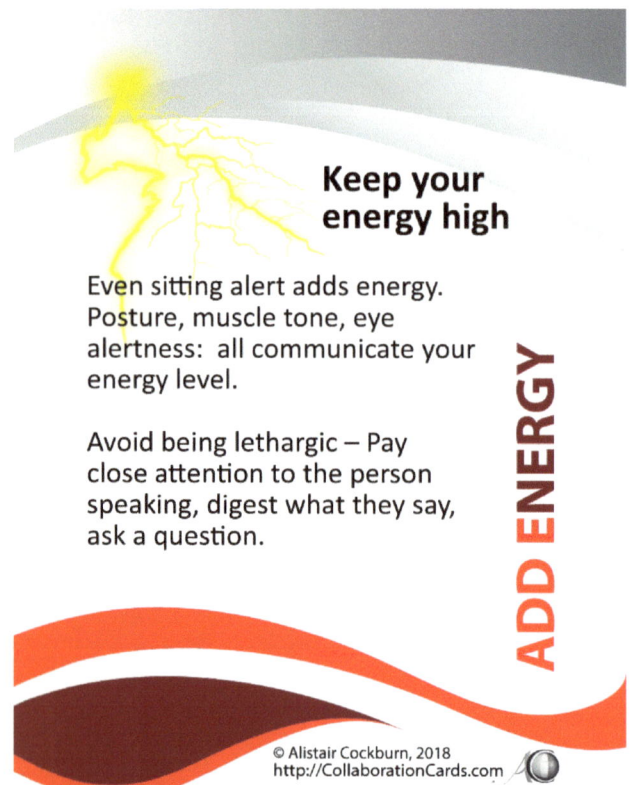

Keep your energy high

Even sitting alert adds energy. Posture, muscle tone, eye alertness: all communicate your energy level.

Avoid being lethargic – Pay close attention to the person speaking, digest what they say, ask a question.

ADD ENERGY

© Alistair Cockburn, 2018
http://CollaborationCards.com

COLLABORATION

The Dance of
Contribution

Add
Energy

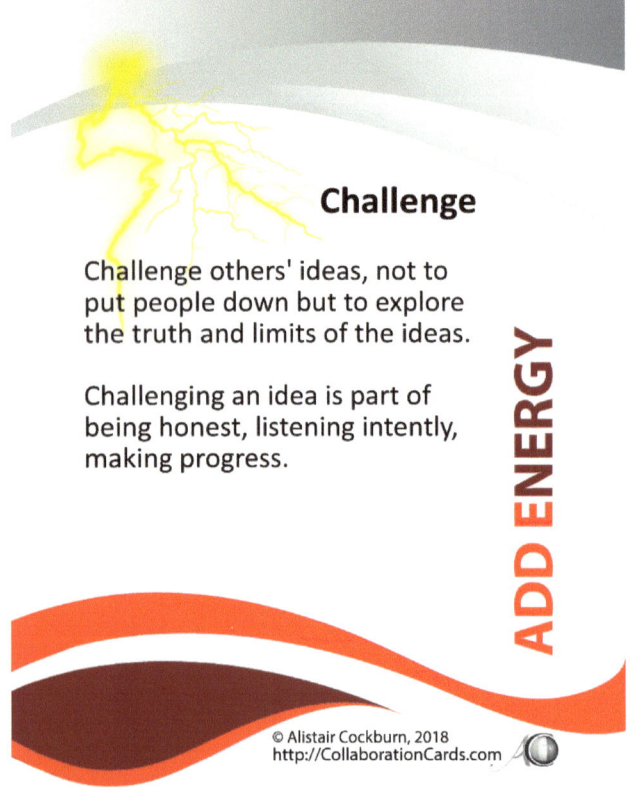

Challenge

Challenge others' ideas, not to put people down but to explore the truth and limits of the ideas.

Challenging an idea is part of being honest, listening intently, making progress.

ADD ENERGY

© Alistair Cockburn, 2018
http://CollaborationCards.com

COLLABORATION

The Dance of Contribution

Add Energy

Make it fun!

Sometimes you can convert a situation to a song, a drawing, a game, making it fun to participate.

When people are having fun, their energy is higher, they participate & collaborate more.

ADD ENERGY

© Alistair Cockburn, 2018
http://CollaborationCards.com

COLLABORATION

The Dance of Contribution

Lift Yourself

Find your center

When you stand in your center, you cannot be moved. You are calm and confident.

Find that place in you, act from there. Your contribution will be easier and have more power.

LIFT YOURSELF

© Alistair Cockburn, 2018
http://CollaborationCards.com

COLLABORATION

The Dance of Contribution

Lift
Yourself

Raise your own sense of power

If you are working with someone you find intimidating, imagine yourself powerful, so you can contribute to this person as an equal.

Pull your shoulders back, take a deep breath in the stomach, imagine what you need, and contribute calmly.

LIFT YOURSELF

© Alistair Cockburn, 2018
http://CollaborationCards.com

Your own card

Start noticing yourself what people do that improves collaboration. Make your own cards! (and write me!)

Fin

Thank you. I hope you use these cards, add your own, and grow this dance of contribution.

About the author

Dr. Alistair Cockburn (pronounced the Scottish way: CO-BURN) is a world-renowned expert on team effectiveness. He is best known for his contributions to the Agile movement including the Heart of Agile. From his decades of experience helping teams of all sizes, his insights are both practical and visionary. He brings the same humanity, clarity, and joy to his books as he does with clients. See more at
https://alistaircockburn.com/.

www.ingramcontent.com/pod-product-compliance
Lightning Source LLC
Chambersburg PA
CBHW040857120626
46551CB00001B/63